Learning How to Learn

EFFECTIVE EDUCATION
PUBLISHING

Printed by
Effective Education Publishing
11755 Riverview Dr.
St. Louis, MO 63138

www.AppliedScholastics.org
Toll-free: 877-75LEARN

ISBN 1-58460-150

© 2006 L. Ron Hubbard Library.
All Rights Reserved.

Any unauthorized copying, translation, duplication, importation or distribution, in whole or in part, by any means, including electronic copying, storage or transmission, is a violation of applicable laws.

Applied Scholastics International is a non-profit educational organization and does not discriminate on the basis of race, color, religion, national origin, sex, disability or age in its programs and activities.

This book is part of the works of L. Ron Hubbard. It is presented to the reader as part of the record of his personal research into life, and the application of the same by others, and should be construed only as a written report of such research and not as a statement of claims made by the author. Any verbal representations made to the contrary are not authorized.

Printed in the United States of America.

APPLIED SCHOLASTICS, Applied Scholastics and Open Book design, EFFECTIVE EDUCATION PUBLISHING and the Effective Education Publishing design are trademarks and service marks owned by Association for Better Living and Education International and are used with its permission.

Item 1134.

CONTENTS

Learning How to Learn	1
Why You Study	17
Trouble with Study	21
Barriers to Study	27
The First Barrier to Study: Lack of Mass	33
The Second Barrier to Study: The Skipped Gradient	49
The Third and Most Important Barrier to Study: The Misunderstood Word	61
Learning the Meanings of Words	85
More About Learning New Words	93
The Eight Steps for Learning the Meaning of a Word	101
Demonstration and Learning	107
Clay Demonstration	113
How to Do a Clay Demo	117
Sketching	123
Summary	133
Congratulations!	135

Part One

LEARNING HOW TO LEARN

LEARNING HOW TO LEARN

You can learn anything you want to learn.

Learning is not just getting more and more facts.

A fact is something that is known to be true.

Getting more and more facts is not learning.

LEARNING HOW TO LEARN COURSE DRILL

Write your answers on a separate sheet of paper. Make sure your name, the date, the name of the course, and the drill number are written on the sheet as well. When finished with this drill, place your paper on the instructor's desk.

DRILL 1-2: Write down five facts about the room you are in.

Learning is understanding new things and getting better ways to do things.

Before you can learn about something, you have to want to learn about that thing.

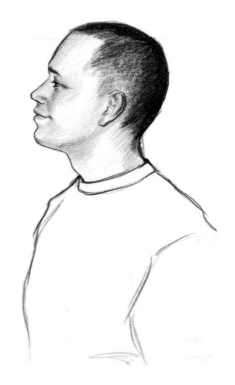

LEARNING HOW TO LEARN COURSE DRILL

Write your answers on a separate sheet of paper. Make sure your name, the date, the name of the course, and the drill number are written on the sheet as well. When finished with this drill, place your paper on the instructor's desk.

DRILL 1-4: What does *learning* mean? Write this down.

DRILL 1-5: Think of some things you would like to learn to do or learn more about. Write these down.

If you think you know all there is to know about something, you will not be able to learn about it.

The first thing you have to decide is that you want to learn something.

He wants to learn.

She wants to learn.

Do *you* want to learn?

LEARNING HOW TO LEARN COURSE DRILL

Write your answers on a separate sheet of paper. Make sure your name, the date, the name of the course, and the drill number are written on the sheet as well. When finished with this drill, place your paper on the instructor's desk.

DRILL 1-7: Make up an example of someone who is studying something, but he feels he already knows about it. What will happen? Write this down.

Once you have decided that there is something you want to learn, the next thing is to study it.

To *study* means to look at something,

and ask about it,

and read about it,

so you learn about it.

LEARNING HOW TO LEARN COURSE DRILL

Write your answers on a separate sheet of paper. Make sure your name, the date, the name of the course, and the drill number are written on the sheet as well. When finished with this drill, place your paper on the instructor's desk.

DRILL 1-9: What does *study* mean? Write this down.

DRILL 1-10: What three things can you do to study something? What is the difference between *study* and *learning*? Write this down.

DRILL 1-11: Name something you want to learn. Write down two ways you could study it.

DRILL 1-12: How could you learn to take care of your body? Write this down.

DRILL 1-13: Choose something you want to learn about. Write down how you would learn about that thing.

WHY YOU STUDY

Many people think that they study so they can pass a test.

But that is not what learning is about.

That is not why you study.

You study to *use* what you have learned.

LEARNING HOW TO LEARN COURSE DRILL

Write your answers on a separate sheet of paper. Make sure your name, the date, the name of the course, and the drill number are written on the sheet as well. When finished with this drill, place your paper on the instructor's desk.

DRILL 1-15: How will you use what you have learned from the last 2 pages? Write this down.

TROUBLE WITH STUDY

Some people do not know how to study so they have trouble learning.

He does not know how to study.

She does not know how to study.

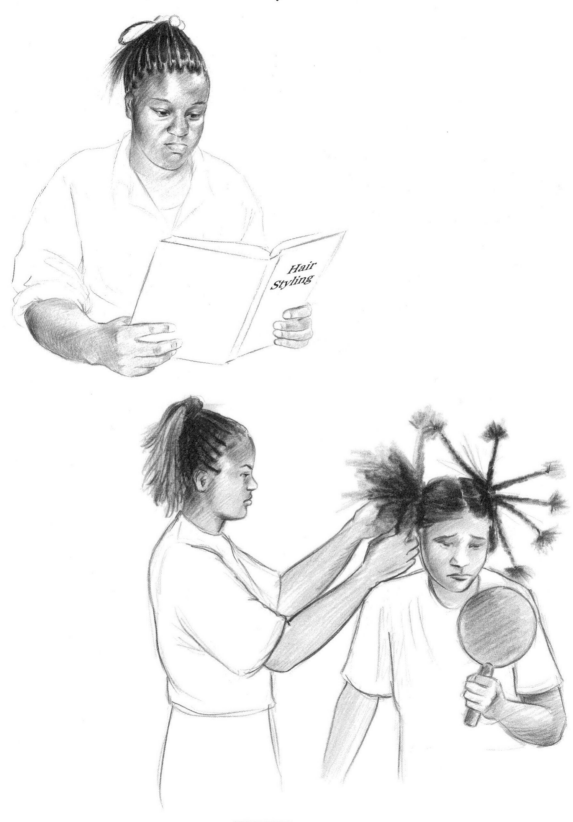

He does not know how to study.

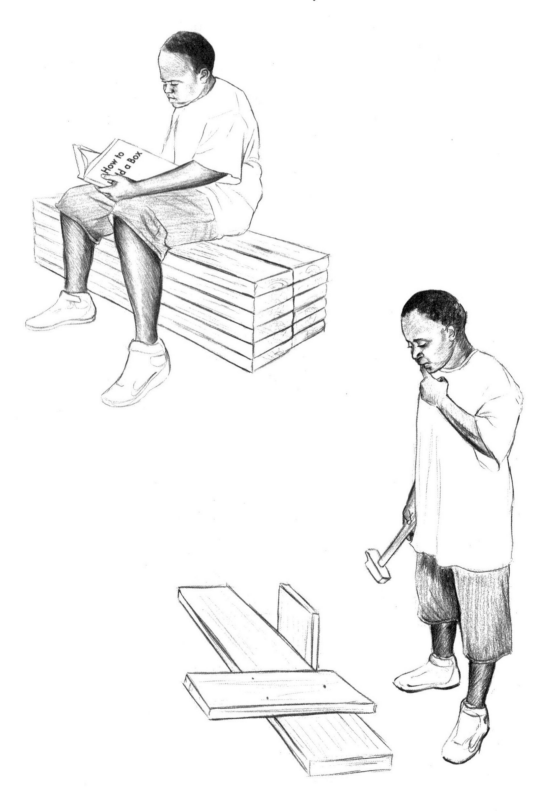

Sometimes you might run into trouble when you are studying and feel like giving up.

If you understand why you run into trouble and you learn how to get out of trouble, you can study easily.

You can get pretty smart!

This book can help you learn how to learn.

It can teach you how to study.

LEARNING HOW TO LEARN COURSE DRILL

Write your answers on a separate sheet of paper. Make sure your name, the date, the name of the course, and the drill number are written on the sheet as well. When finished with this drill, place your paper on the instructor's desk.

DRILL 1-17: Write the answers to the following questions:

a. What would you like to learn about?

b. How would you be helped by learning about that thing?

BARRIERS TO STUDY

When you study, you sometimes run into a *barrier* to learning.

A *barrier* is something that blocks the way or stops you from going on.

If you wanted to learn how to be an electrician,

but you had never seen anyone work with electricity, you might have trouble.

This could be a *barrier* to *study*.

A barrier to study can make learning hard.

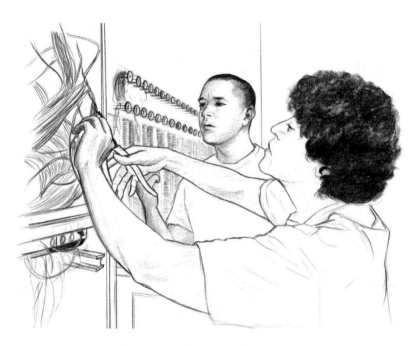

But when you know what the barriers to study are and you can see these barriers and get rid of them, you do not have to be stopped.

You can learn anything you want to learn!

LEARNING HOW TO LEARN COURSE DRILL

Write your answers on a separate sheet of paper. Make sure your name, the date, the name of the course, and the drill number are written on the sheet as well. When finished with this drill, place your paper on the instructor's desk.

DRILL 1-19: What is a *barrier*? Name two things that are barriers. Write these down.

Part Two

THE FIRST BARRIER TO STUDY: LACK OF MASS

THE FIRST BARRIER TO STUDY: LACK OF MASS

The first barrier to study is not having the real thing there that you are studying about.

The real things or the objects that you study about are called *mass*.

If you were studying about cars, you could get the mass of a car by going to a real car and looking at it and touching it.

If you were reading about animals, you could get the mass of animals by going to a zoo or a farm.

LEARNING HOW TO LEARN COURSE DRILL

Write your answers on a separate sheet of paper. Make sure your name, the date, the name of the course, and the drill number are written on the sheet as well. When finished with this drill, place your paper on the instructor's desk.

DRILL 2-3: Walk around the room with someone and point to examples of mass.

DRILL 2-4: How could you get mass if you were studying about cooking? Write this down.

DRILL 2-5: Think of three things you have studied and write them down. Now write what the mass would be for each thing.

DRILL 2-8: With a partner assigned by your instructor, stand up, close your eyes and spin around ONCE as fast as you can. Then open your eyes and look at your partner. Tell your partner how you feel and compare that feeling to the definition of "spinny." If you need to do it again so you notice the feeling, then do so.

DRILL 2-10: With a partner assigned by your instructor, stand up, close your eyes and spin around FIVE TIMES as fast as you can. Then open your eyes and look at your partner. Tell your partner how you feel and compare that feeling to the definition of "dizzy." If you need to do it again so you notice the feeling, then do so.

Studying about something without having the mass of what you are studying can give you trouble.

Studying without the mass of what you are trying to learn can make you feel

squashed,

bent,

or angry.

You can wind up with your stomach feeling funny.

You may get headaches.

You will feel dizzy from time to time

and very often your eyes will hurt.

LEARNING HOW TO LEARN COURSE DRILL

DRILL 2-12: Using your body, demonstrate to someone each of the ways a person can look and feel when they do not have the mass of what they are studying.

The way to stop this from happening is to get the mass of what you are studying.

Sometimes you cannot get the real object you are studying about.

When you cannot get the real thing, pictures help. Movies would help too.

Reading books or listening to someone talk does not give you mass.

Words and talking do not take the place of what you are studying about.

LEARNING HOW TO LEARN COURSE DRILL

Write your answers on a separate sheet of paper. Make sure your name, the date, the name of the course, and the drill number are written on the sheet as well. When finished with this drill, place your paper on the instructor's desk.

DRILL 2-14: Use sheets of paper to do this and give them to your instructor.

Draw a picture of a person feeling:

    a. squashed
    b. bent
    c. spinny
    d. lifeless
    e. bored
    f. angry

DRILL 2-15: Write the answers to the following questions:

a. Why would a person feel the ways listed in the last drill?

b. What would you do to help a person who felt these ways?

DRILL 2-16: Find the mass for each thing listed here and touch it or point to it.

Check off each of the things in the list when you are done.

    a. water
    b. numbers
    c. Earth
    d. people
    e. shoes

DRILL 2-17: For each of these things below, imagine you are studying about it and you don't have the thing there. You start to feel one of the ways you feel when you have lack of mass. For each of these tell someone one or two ways you could get mass. Check off each one when you are done.

    a. a fire station
    b. the President
    c. a football game
    d. a song
    e. the weather
    f. the movies

DRILL 2-18: Imagine you have never seen the color *blue*. Have someone tell you about the color. Then have the person show you something with blue in it. Notice the difference in how you feel about it. Write down how you felt about the color when you were only told about it. Then write down how you felt about the color when you were shown it.

DRILL 2-20: Write down the answers to the questions below.

a. What would you do if you and your brother were in your apartment and he was explaining to you about the engine in an airplane and you started to feel bored and your head started to ache?

b. What would you do if your friend was reading a book about how to use a computer but he felt spinny?

Part Three

THE SECOND BARRIER TO STUDY: THE SKIPPED GRADIENT

THE SECOND BARRIER TO STUDY: THE SKIPPED GRADIENT

A gradient is a way of learning or doing something step by step.

A gradient can be easy and each step can be done easily.

Or a gradient can be hard and each step is difficult to do.

You learn how to do something by learning to do each part of it step by step.

You go through the first step and learn how to do it.

Then you go to the next step and learn how to do that.

You learn how to do each step well and then you can do the whole thing.

Learning something step by step is called learning on a gradient.

If you hit a step that seems too hard to do or you feel you can't understand the step you are on, you have skipped a gradient.

"Skipped" means *left out* or *missed*.

If you don't fully understand a step of something you are learning or you miss a step, you will have a skipped gradient.

Skipping a gradient is a barrier to study.

If you have skipped a gradient you may feel a sort of confusion or reeling.

"Reeling" means having the feeling of your mind going around and around, making it difficult or impossible to go forward with what you are doing.

An example is a person trying to build something. He is confused and sort of reeling.

There was too much of a jump because he did not understand what he was doing,

and he jumped to the next thing and that step was too steep.

He will think his trouble is with his new step.

But it is not.

His trouble is at the end of the step he thought he understood well.

Find out what he thought he understood well just before he got all confused.

You will see he did not really understand that step well.

Get this step understood well,

and he will be able to do the next step.

The gradient is no longer skipped.

LEARNING HOW TO LEARN COURSE DRILL

Write your answers on a separate sheet of paper. Make sure your name, the date, the name of the course, and the drill number are written on the sheet as well. When finished with this drill, place your paper on the instructor's desk.

DRILL 3-3: Write down five examples of things that could bring about a reeling feeling.

DRILL 3-4: Write down the difference between these three reactions: "Sort of spinny," "Dizzy" and "Sort of reeling" noting the barrier to study for each reaction. Get a pass on this from the instructor.

DRILL 3-5: Using your body, demonstrate to someone the two ways a person can feel if they have a skipped gradient when he or she is doing something.

DRILL 3-6: Draw a picture of a person who has a skipped gradient.

DRILL 3-7: Write down the answers to these questions.

a. Why should you learn new things step by step?

b. What can happen if you do not learn things step by step?

DRILL 3-8:

a. Think of a time that you learned something step by step. Write this down.

b. Draw a picture that shows each step that you did.

DRILL 3-9: Think of an example of a skipped gradient. Write this down.

DRILL 3-10: Choose something you can do well, like swimming or playing a game. Imagine someone is learning how to do that. He feels confused and is reeling. Write down what that person should do. In your example tell what action he was doing well on, then where he got confused. Tell where he will find something that he did not really understand. Get a pass on this from the instructor.

Part Four

THE THIRD AND MOST IMPORTANT BARRIER TO STUDY: THE MISUNDERSTOOD WORD

THE THIRD AND MOST IMPORTANT BARRIER TO STUDY: THE MISUNDERSTOOD WORD

The third and most important barrier to study is the *misunderstood word*.

He has a misunderstood word.

"Mis" means *not* or *wrongly*.

"Misunderstood" means *not understood* or *wrongly understood*.

A misunderstood word is a word which is *not understood*,

or a word that is *wrongly understood*.

She has a misunderstood word.

A misunderstood word can be a big word

alphabet

or a small word

him

Have you ever come to the end of a page and realized that you did not remember what you had read?

If you come to the end of a page and do not remember what you have read then there was a word on the page that you did not understand.

Going past a word that you do not understand can make you feel blank,

or tired,

or like you are not there.

You might also feel worried or upset.

LEARNING HOW TO LEARN COURSE DRILL

Write your answers on a separate sheet of paper. Make sure your name, the date, the name of the course, and the drill number are written on the sheet as well. When finished with this drill, place your paper on the instructor's desk.

DRILL 4-4: Write down the differences between "not" and "wrongly" giving examples. Note how you can tell them apart. Get a pass on this from the instructor.

DRILL 4-5: Go through pages 61 to 67 with the instructor. Point out each of the words in the examples that were misunderstood. Tell *how* it was misunderstood. Was it *not understood* or was it *wrongly understood?*

DRILL 4-6: Using your body, demonstrate to someone each of the ways a person can look or feel when he has gone past a misunderstood word.

DRILL 4-7: Draw a picture of a person feeling:

    a. blank
    b. tired
    c. not there
    d. worried and upset

DRILL 4-9: Write down the differences between "angry" and "upset," noting the barrier to study for each reaction. Note how you can tell them apart. Place your paper on the instructor's desk.

These feelings do not happen only when you are reading.

They can also happen when you hear a word you do not understand.

LEARNING HOW TO LEARN COURSE DRILL

Write your answers on a separate sheet of paper. Make sure your name, the date, the name of the course, and the drill number are written on the sheet as well. When finished with this drill, place your paper on the instructor's desk.

DRILL 4-11: Write down the answers to the questions below.

a. Why would a person feel blank or tired or not there while he was studying?

b. If a person felt blank or tired or not there while he was studying, what could you do to help him?

The only reason a person would stop studying or get confused ideas or not be able to learn is because he has passed a word that he did not understand.

A misunderstood word can make you do wrong things.

A misunderstood word can stop you from doing the things you are studying about.

A misunderstood word can make you want to stop studying.

The way to handle this barrier is to look earlier in what you were reading for a misunderstood word.

Go back to before you got into trouble,

find the misunderstood word.

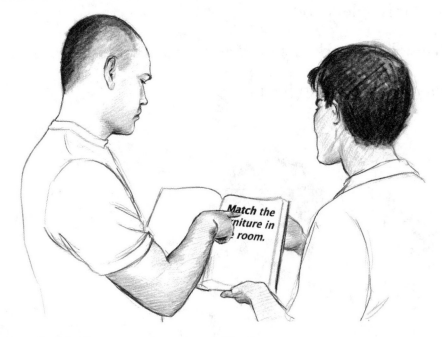

Now look that word up in a dictionary.

A dictionary is a word book. A dictionary is used to find the meanings of words, how to say a word, how to spell a word, how to use a word and many other things about words.

Symbols can be misunderstood in the same way that words can be misunderstood.

A symbol is a mark or sign that means something.

Symbols also need to be understood.

The misunderstood word is the most important of the barriers to study because it is the one that can stop you from learning anything at all.

So if you are feeling blank,

or tired,

or not there,

or worried and upset while you are studying,

it is *always* because of a misunderstood word or symbol.

LEARNING HOW TO LEARN COURSE DRILL

Write your answers on a separate sheet of paper. Make sure your name, the date, the name of the course, and the drill number are written on the sheet as well. When finished with this drill, place your paper on the instructor's desk.

DRILL 4-14: You are reading a book at home. You get to the bottom of a page but you do not remember what the page was about. Why would this happen? Write down your answer.

DRILL 4-15: Explain why the misunderstood word is the most important barrier to study. Write this down.

DRILL 4-16: Think of a time when you observed someone have this barrier. Write this down.

DRILL 4-17: Using your body, demonstrate to another person each of the additional ways a person can look or feel when he has gone past a misunderstood word.

Part Five

LEARNING THE MEANINGS OF WORDS

LEARNING HOW TO LEARN COURSE DRILL

Write your answers on a separate sheet of paper. Make sure your name, the date, the name of the course, and the drill number are written on the sheet as well. When finished with this drill, place your paper on the instructor's desk.

DRILL 5-2: Remember a time you knew something completely and could do it VERY well. Remember how you felt. Remember another time you knew something completely and could do it VERY well. Again remember how you felt. Compare how you felt to the definition of "bright." Write down your observations. Get a pass on this from the instructor.

DRILL 5-3: Remember a time you sort of knew something and couldn't do it very well or couldn't do it at all. Remember how you felt at the time. Compare how you felt to the definition of "bright." Write down your observations. Get a pass on this from the instructor.

DRILL 5-4: Write down what "bright" means in your own words. Get a pass on this from the instructor.

LEARNING THE MEANINGS OF WORDS

If you are studying and do not feel as bright as you did,

or if you are taking too long on what you are studying,

or you are yawning,

or doodling,

or daydreaming,

you have gone past a misunderstood word.

If you have a misunderstood word, there are some steps you need to do.

1. Look earlier in your book and find the word you do not understand.

2. Find the word in a dictionary.

3. Look over all of the definitions. A definition tells you the meaning of a word. Find the definition that fits what you were reading.

4. Read this definition.

5. Make up sentences using the word that way until you really understand that definition. You might have to make up many sentences. Maybe ten or more.

That is okay.

The important thing is that you understand what the word means.

6. When you understand the definition that fits in what you were reading, then learn each of the other definitions the same way.

7. After you learn all of the definitions of that word then go back to what you were reading. If you are not bright and ready to study again, then there is still another word that you do not understand.

Do steps 1 through 7 again until you are bright and ready to study again.

8. Then start studying from the place where the misunderstood word was.

(If you found more than one misunderstood word, start studying again from the place where you found the earliest misunderstood word.)

LEARNING HOW TO LEARN COURSE DRILL

Write your answers on a separate sheet of paper. Make sure your name, the date, the name of the course, and the drill number are written on the sheet as well. When finished with this drill, place your paper on the instructor's desk.

DRILL 5-6: Find the word "chicken" in a dictionary. Find the right definition for "chicken" as it is used in this sentence: *The chicken lived in the barn with the rest of the animals.* Show another person how you would learn what the word "chicken" means by doing the steps of how to learn the meaning of a word.

DRILL 5-8: Show the instructor how you would find a misunderstood word in something you are reading.

MORE ABOUT LEARNING NEW WORDS

Sometimes when groups of words are used together, these words do not mean the same things as they do all by themselves.

For example, here is a sentence: "The singer's performance will bring the house down." "Bring the house down" means *to get very loud applause*. It does not mean that the singer is going to lower a house using a crane. When words are used like this it is called an *idiom*.

"Bring the house down" does not mean this:

"Bring the house down" means this:

Have you heard a person say, "Shake a leg?"

"Shake a leg" does *not* mean that you should shake your leg.

"Shake a leg" means *to dance*.

"Shake a leg" can also mean *to hurry*.

Dictionaries show the idioms of a word after the definitions of a word.

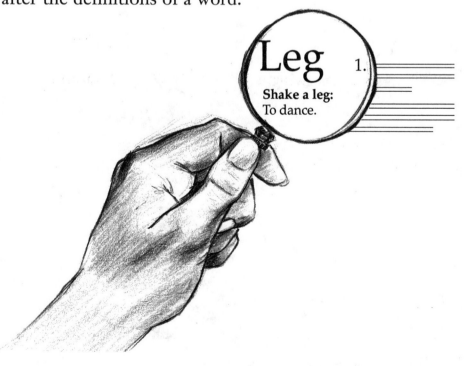

If you are learning a word that has idioms you should learn the idioms after the other definitions of the word.

Use the idioms in sentences just like you do when you are learning the other definitions of a word.

LEARNING HOW TO LEARN COURSE DRILL

Write your answers on a separate sheet of paper. Make sure your name, the date, the name of the course, and the drill number are written on the sheet as well. When finished with this drill, place your paper on the instructor's desk.

DRILL 5-10: Read the further examples of idioms in the glossary. Write down what an idiom is, giving examples. Write down the steps of how to learn idioms.

DRILL 5-11: Look up the word "heart" in your dictionary and learn all the idioms. (If your dictionary doesn't have idioms, have the instructor help you find at least one idiom for "heart.")

When you are learning a word, you may find a word in the definition that you do not understand.

Find that word in the dictionary too, and learn all of its definitions.

Then go back to the first word you were learning.

When you understand all the words in what you are studying you can understand the whole thing.

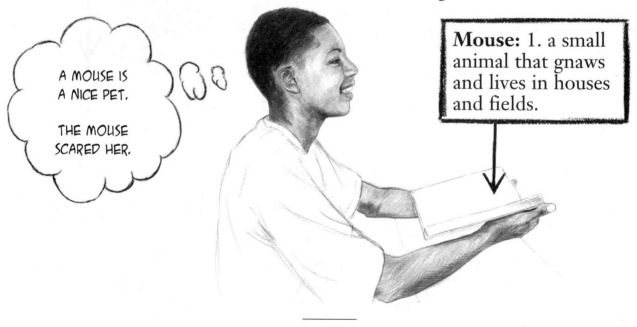

THE EIGHT STEPS FOR LEARNING THE MEANING OF A WORD

1. Look earlier in your book and find the word you do not understand.

2. Find the word in a dictionary.

3. Look over all of the definitions. A definition tells you the meaning of a word. Find the definition that fits what you were reading.

4. Read this definition.

5. Make up sentences using the word that way until you really understand that definition. You might have to make up many sentences. Maybe ten or more.

   That is okay.

   The important thing is that you understand what the word means.

6. When you understand the definition that fits in what you were reading, then learn each of the other definitions the same way.

7. After you learn all of the definitions of that word then go back to what you were reading. If you are

not bright and ready to study again, then there is still another word that you do not understand.

Do steps 1 through 7 again until you are bright and ready to study again.

8. Then start studying from the place where the misunderstood word was.

    (If you found more than one misunderstood word, start studying again from the place where you found the earliest misunderstood word.)

LEARNING HOW TO LEARN COURSE DRILL

Write your answers on a separate sheet of paper. Make sure your name, the date, the name of the course, and the drill number are written on the sheet as well. When finished with this drill, place your paper on the instructor's desk.

DRILL 5-13: Suppose you are learning the definitions of a new word. You find a word in a definition that you don't understand. Show the instructor what you should do.

DRILL 5-14: Find a word in something you are studying that you do not know the meaning of. Use a dictionary to find out what that word means using the eight steps of how to learn the meaning of a word.

DRILL 5-15: Practice saying the eight steps until you can say them easily. You can use your own words. Say these to the instructor in your own words.

DRILL 5-16:

a. Find another word in something you are studying that you do not know the meaning of. Use a dictionary to find out what that word means using the eight steps of how to learn the meaning of a word.

b. Repeat the above with other words that you don't understand until you can do all the steps easily.

Part Six

DEMONSTRATION AND LEARNING

DEMONSTRATION AND LEARNING

The word "demonstrate" means to show, or to show how something works. A *demonstration* is something done to show something or how it works.

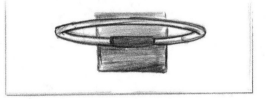

Doing a demonstration is a good way to teach someone something. Demonstration is an important part of learning.

When you are studying, you can do a "demonstration" or "demo" with a demo kit. A demo kit is made of different objects such as corks, pen tops, buttons, pieces of sponge or other similar things. You can demonstrate an idea or rule or anything you are studying with your hands and the pieces of your demo kit.

This is a demo kit.

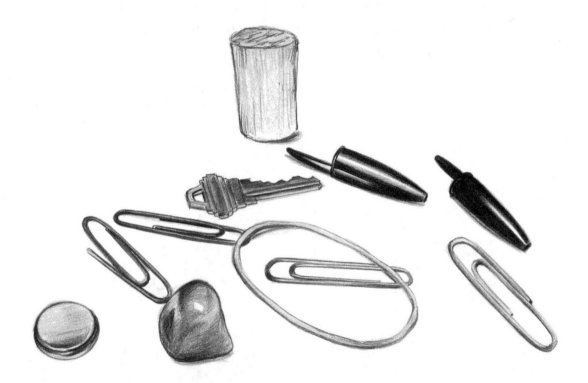

If you ran into something you could not figure out, a demo kit would help you to understand it. You can make different pieces of the demo kit take the place of the things you are studying about. You can move the objects around to see how something works. By doing this you are getting *mass* that helps you understand the ideas you are studying about.

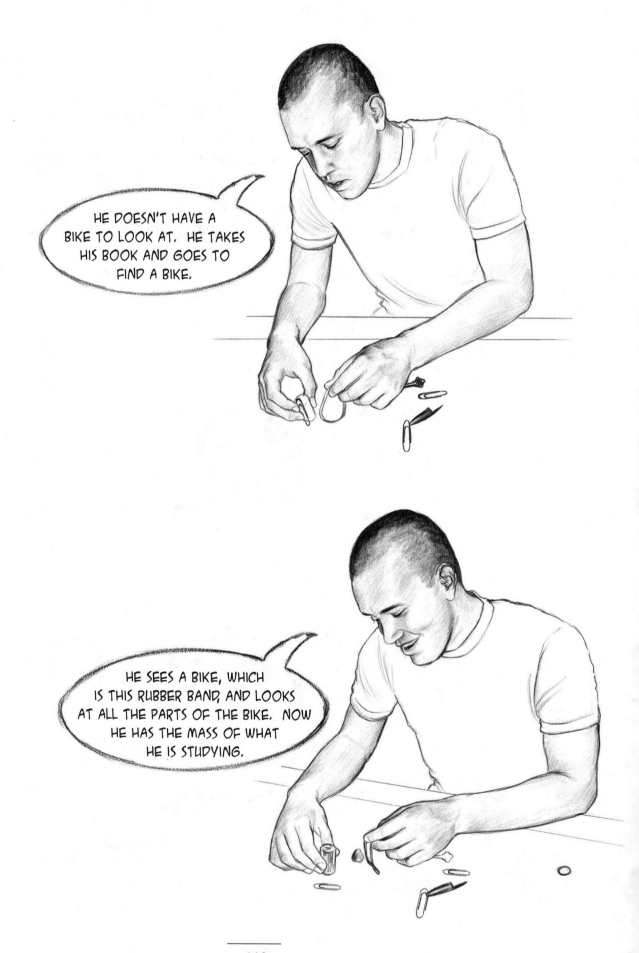

LEARNING HOW TO LEARN COURSE DRILL

Write your answers on a separate sheet of paper. Make sure your name, the date, the name of the course, and the drill number are written on the sheet as well. When finished with this drill, place your paper on the instructor's desk.

DRILL 6-2: Make a demo kit for yourself.

DRILL 6-3: Using your demo kit, show another person how you would get from where you are to the bathroom. Have the instructor watch you do this.

DRILL 6-4: Using your demo kit, demonstrate the first barrier to study to another person. Then demonstrate how you would help someone who has the first barrier to study.

DRILL 6-5: Using your demo kit, demonstrate the second barrier to study to another person. Then demonstrate how you would help someone who has the second barrier to study.

DRILL 6-6: Using your demo kit, demonstrate the third barrier to study to another person. Then demonstrate how you would help someone who has the third barrier to study.

DRILL 6-7: Why would you do a demo when you are studying? Write down the answer.

DRILL 6-8: Imagine you are learning to be a taxi-driver. You need to drive from one place in the city to another place. Show how you can use a demo kit to help work it out and have the mass on it. Have the instructor watch you do this.

CLAY DEMONSTRATION

Another way to demonstrate what you are studying is to make it in clay.

This is called a "clay demonstration" or "clay demo." Demonstrating something in clay can help you to figure out how something is put together, how it looks or how it works. It can help you understand better what you are studying.

If you come across something you cannot figure out, you can work it out in clay.

There are many ways that clay can be used.

People who design new cars make clay models of cars to see how they will look.

A general will make a model of the battlefield so he can get an idea of how to win the battle.

You can understand *anything* better by demonstrating it in clay. If you wanted to figure out how to organize your room better so you could fit a new desk in it, you could make a model of the room and the furniture and other things. Then you could move them around and find the best way to arrange them.

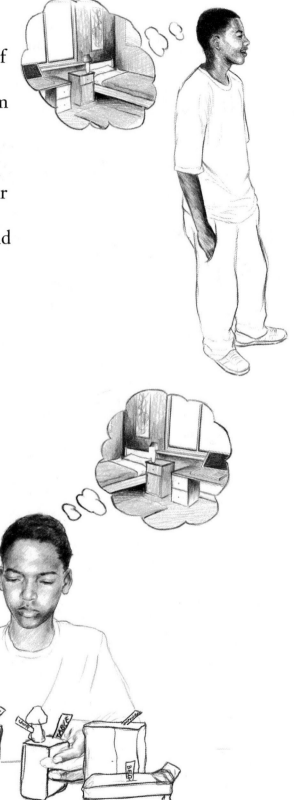

HOW TO DO A CLAY DEMO

Clay demos are done using clay to make the mass of the thing. Then a label is made to say what the thing is. Let's see how this works.

If you want to do a clay demo of a pencil, first make a thin piece of clay. This is the pencil lead. Then make a label that says "LEAD" and stick it on the thin roll of clay.

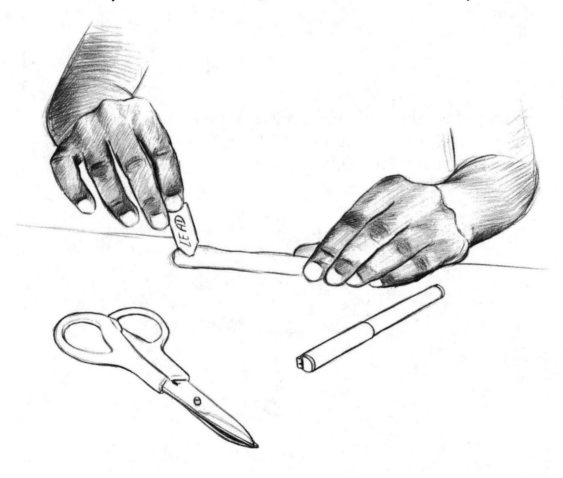

Next, put another layer of clay with the thin roll sticking out a little bit at one end.

This is the wood part of the pencil, so you would make a label that says "WOOD" and stick it on.

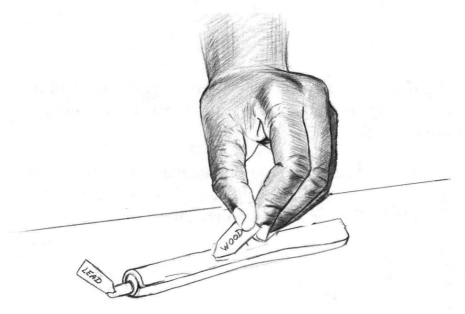

Then put another little piece of clay on the end. This is the rubber eraser, so you would label it "RUBBER" and stick it on that piece of clay.

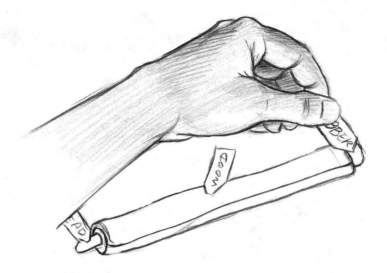

Finally, you make a label for the whole thing. This label says "PENCIL."

Clay demos must be large. If a clay demo is too small it might not make what you are studying real enough. Making the things you are studying in clay can help make them more *real* to you.

Making BIG clay demos works better to help you understand what you are studying.

Even a thought can be shown in clay. You can use a thin piece of clay to show a thought or idea. Here is a clay demo of a person thinking about a ball.

If you don't understand something in life you can work it out in clay and understand it better. *Anything* can be shown in clay.

Clay demos are an important part of learning how to learn.

LEARNING HOW TO LEARN COURSE DRILL

Write your answers on a separate sheet of paper. Make sure your name, the date, the name of the course, and the drill number are written on the sheet as well. When finished with this drill, place your paper on the instructor's desk.

DRILL 6-10: Using your demo kit, show *when* you put the labels on when you are doing a clay demo. Show this to the instructor.

DRILL 6-11: Do a clay demo of a shoe. Have the instructor give you a pass on this.

DRILL 6-12: Do a clay demo of a person thinking about a shoe. Have the instructor give you a pass on this.

DRILL 6-13: Imagine you were reading how to build a house. Do a clay demonstration that could help you build the house or some part of it. Show your demonstration to the instructor once this is done.

SKETCHING

A sketch is a rough drawing of something.

Sketching is also a part of demonstration and part of working things out.

You sometimes see people doing sketching at work. They work things out for themselves by sketching it.

LEARNING HOW TO LEARN COURSE DRILL

Write your answers on a separate sheet of paper. Make sure your name, the date, the name of the course, and the drill number are written on the sheet as well. When finished with this drill, place your paper on the instructor's desk.

DRILL 6-15: Do a sketch of how to get from where you are to the dining area.

Part Seven

USING THE INFORMATION

LEARNING HOW TO LEARN COURSE DRILL

Write your answers on a separate sheet of paper. Make sure your name, the date, the name of the course, and the drill number are written on the sheet as well. When finished with this drill, place your paper on the instructor's desk.

DRILL 7-1: List all the ways you can feel if you have lack of mass. Show the list to the instructor when you have done this to make sure it is complete.

DRILL 7-2: List all of the ways you can feel if you skip a gradient. Show the list to the instructor when you have done this to make sure it is complete.

DRILL 7-3: List all of the ways you can feel if you go past a word you don't understand. Show the list to the instructor when you have done this to make sure it is complete.

DRILL 7-4: Use your demo kit and show how you can feel when you have skipped a gradient. Show this to the instructor.

DRILL 7-5: Sketch all the ways you can feel when you have lack of mass. Get a pass on this from the instructor.

DRILL 7-6: With your body, demonstrate five of the ways you can feel when you have a misunderstood word. Get a pass on this from the instructor.

DRILL 7-7: For this drill get the study drill cards from the instructor.

The front of the cards have all the ways a person can feel when he has a barrier to study. The back of the cards have the name of the barrier to study and the ways to handle it.

a) Drill by yourself with the cards until you can look at the way a person can feel on the front of the card and then from memory say the right barrier to study and the ways to handle it. If the ways to handle the barrier have numbered steps, then you need to be able to say them in the right order.

b) For the second part of the drill, the instructor will have another person act as a helper. The helper mixes the cards and stacks them all facing the same way.

The helper holds up the first card. You see the side showing how the person feels. The helper sees the side that has the barrier and the ways to handle it.

Look at the first card. Read aloud the way a person can feel.

Say the right barrier to study and the ways to handle it. Use your own words. The answer is right if you say the right barrier and all the ways to handle it. If there are steps with numbers, you need to give them in order.

If you give the right answer, the helper says "good" and puts the first card in a pile.

If you don't give the right answer, the helper shows you the right answer and tells you what you said wrong. Read the right answer aloud.

That card goes to the back of the stack so you can do it again.

Do this for all the cards.

Do this drill over and over. When you can easily say the right barrier and the ways to handle it, get the instructor to check you on this. When you go through the cards with no mistakes, you have passed the drill.

DRILL 7-8: Why will it help you to know how to study? Write this down.

SUMMARY

People who do well in life never really stop studying and learning. There are a lot of things to learn.

Learning is not hard to do and it can be enjoyable.

Now that you know the barriers to study and how to handle them, you can learn anything you want to learn.

And you can help others learn too.

CONGRATULATIONS!

You have completed the Applied Scholastics *Learning How to Learn* Course.

Knowing how to learn is useful and important. It is very well done that you have learned this.

Have fun applying your new skills to anything you study. That is what they are there for!

GLOSSARY

angry: the feeling one gets when he or she is very mad about something. *Examples: The driver became* angry *when there was so much traffic. When her friend didn't call on time, she was* angry.

applied: put into use. *Example: The new cook* applied *what she had learned about baking and made a wonderful cake.*

barrier: something that blocks the way or stops you from going on. *Examples: Without a key, the locked door was a* barrier. *The fact that the student had only slept 4 hours was a* barrier *to his understanding of the new subject.*

based on: what something comes from. *Example: The movie was* based on *a bestselling book.*

bent: curved or crooked, not straight. *Examples: The student was* bent *over his desk. The ball player* bent *to get the ball.*

blank: having a feeling of being empty because you are empty of any thoughts. *Example: While he was giving his friend the directions, Sam went* blank *on the name of the store.*

bored: a feeling one gets when he or she is not interested in anything in particular. *Example: The class was* bored *with the subject. The children were* bored *and asked their mother what they could do.*

bright: when you are clear about something, can understand it and do well with it, you are feeling bright. *Examples: After learning how to solve the problem, she felt* bright. *After several tries, he finally understood how to put the engine back together and had a* bright *feeling.*

Certificates and Awards: the person or area that makes sure each student can apply what they have learned and gives a certificate (piece of paper) as an award to those who have completed the course. *Example: The student completed the course and was given a course certificate by Tim who works in the* Certificates and Awards *area.*

checksheet: a list of all of the actions one needs to do on a course, listed in the order they are to be done. Different checksheets cover different things. *Example: After he did each item on the* checksheet, *in order, he had learned how to fix the brakes on his car.*

clay demonstration/clay demo: a form of demonstration where you use clay (with labels) to show the thing or idea you are demonstrating. Demonstrating something in clay can help you to figure out how something is put together, how it looks or how it works. It can help you understand better what you are studying. *Example: Once she did a* clay demo *showing what happens when you go by a word you do not know or fully understand, she began looking up her words all the time.*

clear: to remove any uncertainties or confusions about something so it is fully understood. *Example: She* cleared *her words in music and found she improved her piano playing.*

come across: to find or meet unexpectedly. *Example: While walking in town, you may* come across *people from many different countries.*

confusion: when something is mixed up or not clear to you, it is a confusion. *Example: The* confusion *he felt went away after he realized he was missing a piece to the puzzle.*

congratulations: a word said to someone after they have done something special or have done something very well and you want to show that you are happy about it, too. *Example:* Congratulations *on completing the course!*

course: all of the material one studies and drills to learn how to do something. *Examples: He took a* course *to learn how to communicate. She took a* course *to learn how to fix the brakes of her car.*

course administrator: the person who handles all the paperwork and materials of the course and keeps things organized for the instructor. *Example: The* course administrator *filed all the completed checksheets in the student files.*

data: information about something. *Example: The* data *about fire prevention was important to know.*

daydreaming: thinking about other things that are pleasant and not paying attention to what is happening around you. *Example: She was* daydreaming *about going on vacation and missed everything the teacher was talking about.*

definition: the meaning of a word. *Example: It was amazing to him how many* definitions *there are for the word "run."*

demo: a shorter way of saying the word "demonstration." *Example: When I couldn't understand how all the parts fit together, I did a* demo *of each one and then it made sense.*

demo kit: different objects such as corks, caps, paper clips, pen tops, rubber bands or other things. You can demonstrate an idea or rule or anything you are studying with your hands and the pieces of your demo kit. By doing this you get "mass" that helps you understand the ideas you are studying about. *Example: He showed me how to make my own* demo kit *at the dinner table with the salt and pepper shakers, packets of sugar, forks and spoons.*

demonstrate: to show something or to show how something works. *Example: I asked the teacher to* demonstrate *how to solve the problem.*

demonstration: something done to show something or to show how it works. *Examples: The* demonstration *of how to juggle 3 balls was very fun to watch. Using her demo kit, the student did a* demonstration *of how to do laundry.*

dictionary: a book that tells you the meanings of words, how to say a word, how to spell a word, how to use a word and many other things about words. *Example: Every student needs a good* dictionary *in order to study.*

dizzy: having a feeling of not being able to balance yourself; unsteady or feeling like you are losing your balance. *Examples: I was* dizzy *after trying to keep up with the directions from the store manager. He felt* dizzy *after the roller-coaster ride.*

doodling: scribbling or drawing without giving any real attention or thought to what you are drawing. *Example: She was* doodling *while talking on the phone.*

drill: the way to learn something by practicing. *Example: He did the* drill *several times until he could do it easily.* Also, to do something over and over again until you can do it well. *Example: The pilot will* drill *the procedures so he knows them without ever thinking about them.*

education: the action of learning information and skills to help you do things in life. *Example: He never stopped his* education *because he continued to learn all through his life.*

effective: producing the intended result. *Example: He was an* effective *coach and his team brought home the championship.*

fact: something that is known to be true. *Example: The* fact *was that the game was over and we won!*

from time to time: sometimes; now and then; not all of the time. *Example:* From time to time *I like to eat vanilla ice cream instead of chocolate.*

funny: feeling strange; feeling slightly ill. *Example: The boy felt* funny *after his father spun him around.*

general: a high-ranking military officer. *Example: The general told the soldiers to retreat.*

get rid of: to make something go away. *Example: I couldn't figure out how to get rid of the smell in the trashcan.*

give up: to no longer try or make an effort. *Example: Although the young girl was not good at mathematics, her teacher told her not to give up.*

gradient: something done or learned step by step. *Examples: He taught with an easy gradient to learn how to juggle. The instructions did not give the right gradient to put the bookshelf together.*

headache: pain in one's head. *Example: I had a headache after forgetting to eat dinner last night.*

hit: to arrive at or come into contact with. *Example: The man was building a house and hit a step that was too difficult.*

idiom: sometimes when words are used together, these words do not mean the same thing as they do all by themselves. When words are used in this way, it is called an idiom. *Examples: "bring the house down" means to receive very loud applause. It is an idiom because it does not mean that you will "move the house lower." "Hit the road" means to get going to some place; to leave or depart. It is an idiom because it does not mean that you will "go strike the road with your hand or an object." To "crack the case" is an idiom that means the crime has been solved. It does <u>not</u> mean what the words would usually mean (to put a crack into a case).*

initial: to write the first letters of one's first and last names on the checksheet line to show that you have fully completed that step. *Example: Once you pass the drill, your instructor will initial that line on your checksheet.*

instructor: an individual trained to help students to learn to apply the material on their course. An Instructor does not teach. An Instructor is there to help the students understand the material so they can apply it. *Example: The student raised his hand for the* Instructor *the minute he ran into trouble.*

instructor pass: when the instructor checks your ability to do a drill or your understanding of information to make sure you can use it. *Examples: After drilling with his coach, the student raised his hand for an* instructor pass. *As part of the* Instructor Pass, *he was asked to demonstrate how he would use the information.*

jump: a sudden rise or increase. *Examples: There was a huge* jump *in sales this month. The temperature took a big* jump *overnight — from 60° to 80°.*

lack: without or not enough (of something). *Examples: The bakery closed because of a* lack *of flour. A* lack *of rain made the lawn turn brown.*

learning: understanding new things and getting better ways to do things. *Examples: She had fun* learning *about sharks and the sea. The cook was excited about* learning *from the top chef.*

lifeless: not being lively or active; when you feel as if you have no energy. *Example: After losing another game, the team felt and looked* lifeless.

mass: the real things or objects that one is studying about. *Examples: If you are studying about cars, the* mass *will be one or more cars. Going on the field trip to the restaurant gave the students lots of* mass *on how a restaurant works.*

materials: the writings, objects and other parts of a course, which make up the information and skills one is learning. *Example: His course* materials *to learn how to use the telephone included his checksheet, his course manual and the telephone instruction book.*

mis-: not or wrongly. *Examples: The water gun* mis*fired and no water came out. She* mis*read the sign and took a wrong turn. She* mis*spelled the word.*

misunderstood: not understood or wrongly understood. *Example: She* misunderstood *the directions on the medicine bottle, took too much and got sicker.*

misunderstood word: a word which is not understood or a word which is wrongly understood. *Example: She had a* misunderstood word *in the recipe and that was the reason she could not get the cake to taste like her grandmother's.*

no longer: not anymore; not now. *Example: It is* no longer *raining outside.*

not: in no way. *Examples: She did* not *get to the bus before it left. He will* not *be on time.*

not there: not thinking about or listening to what one is supposed to be thinking or listening to, but thinking about something else instead. *Examples: If you are* not there, *you are not aware of what is going on around you. As he was* not there, *he missed what was being said and done.*

pass: when you complete a checkout, you are told it is a pass; when a drill has been done correctly and the student has had a very good win, it is a pass. *Example: Both students had worked very hard to get their* pass *and felt proud now that they had passed.*

publishing: the actions to get written material out to the public. *Example: He worked very hard on the* publishing *of the daily newspaper.*

purpose: the reason for something; what one wants to do. *Example: His* purpose *in coming to the course was to improve his communication skills.*

reeling: having the feeling of one's mind going around and around, making it difficult or impossible to move forward with action. Also moving or swaying like you might fall. *Example: The beginning diver found herself* reeling *as she stepped out onto the high diving platform.*

rough drawing: a very simple drawing, not like one that an artist would do. *Example: I did a* rough drawing *of a map along with the directions so they would not get lost.*

rubber: material used to make things like tires, rubber bands, erasers and things like this. It can stretch and bend easily without breaking. *Example: The eraser on the pencil was made of* rubber.

run into: to come to something; to be up against something unexpectedly. *Example: I didn't want to* run into *that problem anymore.*

run into trouble: to come to something that is hard or difficult to understand—it causes you trouble. *Example: If you go by words you do not understand, you will* run into trouble.

scholastics: schooling and education. *Example: The subject of* scholastics *is made up of everything having to do with education.*

sign-off: to put your initials and the date on something. *Example: Once you pass the drill, your twin will* sign-off *that line on your checksheet.*

sketch: a rough (very simply done) drawing of something. Sketching is one of the ways to demonstrate something. *Example: I asked him to* sketch *the best way to fix the pipe.*

skipped: left out or missed. *Example: The child* skipped *breakfast.*

skipped gradient: something not done or learned step by step. One of the steps of learning something has been left out or skipped, so you do not fully understand it. *Example: When the student couldn't play the new piece of music, he knew he had a* skipped gradient.

sort of: a little like or kind of like (something). *Example: When meeting new people, the little girl was* sort of *shy but was always polite.*

sort of spinny: a little like having the feeling that one has after (or as one is) turning around and around. *Example: He was listening to a lecture about trees and found he felt* sort of spinny.

spinny: to feel like you are turning around and around. *Examples: His head felt* spinny *after being lost for an hour. When he twirled her on the dance floor, she felt* spinny.

squashed: pushed down smaller and not in the normal shape. *Example: The students looked* squashed *after listening to the teacher read from the book.*

steep: going up too high all at once, not going up easily step by step. *Example: The students found the hill very* steep *and very hard to climb.*

step-by-step: done one step at a time; first doing one step, then doing the next step, then the next step, etc. *Example: They learned the dance by doing it* step-by-step.

stomach feeling funny: when your stomach hurts or feels upset or you have a sick feeling in your stomach. *Example: The student complained about his* stomach feeling funny *during math class.*

study: to look at something, ask about it and read about it, so you learn about it. *Example: She decided to* study *cameras.*

summary: the important parts of something briefly said or written. *Example: Some textbooks give a* summary *at the end of each chapter.*

suppose: to imagine or think of as possible. *Example: Suppose you win the lottery, what will you buy first?*

symbol: a mark or sign that replaces or stands for something else. *Examples: a plus sign (+), a period (.) and a comma (,) are all* symbols.

tag end: the last or final part of something. *Example: The* tag end *of the movie was the best.*

tired: feeling like you can't continue because you need to rest; feeling like you have little or no energy. *Example: After carrying the piano up the stairs, he was very* tired *and sat down to rest.*

trouble: difficulties; misunderstandings. *Example: I had* trouble *with my homework and had to get help.*

understand: to know what is meant; to know the meaning of. *Example: It is very important that a student does not go by a word he does not fully* understand *without finding out what the word means.*

upset: feeling troubled or uneasy or worried. *Examples: I was* upset *when I realized the money was not in my pocket. The girl was* upset *when she was late for the appointment.*

use: to put it into practice or to put it into action. *Example: It was time to* use *my speaking skills and make an announcement to the group.*

wind up: to come to be in a certain situation as a result of something. *Example: If you quit your job, you may* wind up *with no money.*

worried: concerned, nervous or troubled about something. *Examples: I was* worried *when they didn't arrive to pick me up. She searched for the child and became* worried *when she didn't find her right away.*

wrongly: not in a right way; not correctly. *Examples: He entered the phone number* wrongly. *They* wrongly *understood the directions and got lost.*

Applied Scholastics International

International Training Center — Corporate Headquarters
11755 Riverview Drive, St. Louis, Missouri 63138 USA
Tel: 314 355 6355   Fax: 314 355 2621

Continental and National Offices

Education Alive Africa
PO Box 30791
Kyalami 1684
South Africa
+2711 702 2208
educalive@yebo.co.za

**Applied Scholastics
Australia, New Zealand
& Oceania**
1/2 Avona, Avona Ave.
Glebe 2037
New South Wales
Australia
+6129 569 9562
apsanzo@AppliedScholastics.org

Applied Scholastics Canada
25 Mathieu.
Saint-Basile-le-Grand, Qc
J3N 1H2
Canada
+1 450 461 9541
apscanada@AppliedScholastics.org

Applied Scholastics CIS
B. Pereyaslavskaya Str. 11
129110 Moscow, Russia
+7 095 5078709
info@apscis.ru

**Applied Scholastics
Czech Republic**
Opletalova 36
Prague 1, 110 00
Czech Republic
+420 222 246 605
AppliedScholastics@tiscali.cz

**Applied Scholastics
Denmark**
Nørregade 26
1165 Copenhagen K
Denmark
+45 33 32 36 80
hanne@apseu.dk

**Applied Scholastics
Eastern United States, USA**
1255 Cleveland Street
Suite 100
Clearwater, FL 33755
+1 727 432 3233
euscontrep@AppliedScholastics.org

Applied Scholastics Europe
Nørregade 26
1165 Copenhagen K
Denmark
+45 33 32 36 80
apseu@AppliedScholastics.org

Applied Scholastics France
c/o: Marie Therese Brunet
53, Ave. Marcel Sembat
93190 Livry-Gargan
France
+33 1430 18415
matenebru@netcourrier.com

**Applied Scholastics
Germany**
Grosser Weg 3
30826 Garbsen
Germany
+49 5131 447 247
kathirunge@yahoo.de

Applied Scholastics Greece
c/o: Kelly Laoumtzis
Megalou Alexandrou 72
Nea Smyrni
17122 Athens, Greece
+30 2109 325 400
keyelart@hotmail.com

**Applied Scholastics
Hungary**
Erzsébet Ter 16
8800 Nagykanizsa
Hungary
+3630 900 3488
alkalmazottoktatastan.kht@chello.hu

**Applied Scholastics
Indonesia**
Jl. Slamet Riyadi no 16
Jakarta 13150, Indonesia
+62218583077
Fax +62218511423
aps_indonesia@yahoo.co.id

**Applied Scholastics
Italy & Mediterraneo**
Via Leoncavallo 8
Milano 20131
Italy
+39 022 85 10 139
apsitl@interfree.it

Applied Scholastics Jamaica
Shop #5, Begonia Lg. Plaza
Linstead, Box 45, Ewarton
St. Catherine, Jamaica, W.I.
+1 876 903-1990
AppliedScholasticsja@yahoo.com

Applied Scholastics Japan
1-1 Ishikawa-Higashionna
Uruma City
Okinawa 904-1111
Japan
+81 098-965-7072
japan@tsukaeru.org
okinawa@tsukaeru.org

**Applied Scholastics
Latin America**
Rio Elba 10 Int. 101-A
Cuauhtemoc, Cuauhtemoc
Mexico D.F. 06500
Mexico
+5255 5211 8452
info@apslatam.org

Applied Scholastics Latvia
Abavas Str. 21
Riga LV-1004
Latvia
+371 727 1452
soldi@inbox.lv

**Applied Scholastics
Malaysia**
15 Lorong Bukit Raja
Taman Seputeh
Kuala Lumpur, 58000
Malaysia
+603 2274 5747
apsmal@po.jaring.my

**Applied Scholastics
New Zealand**
13 Sutton Crescent
PO Box 63052
Papatoetoe, Auckland
New Zealand
+649 278 4077
rule_education@msn.com

Applied Scholastics Sweden
Kallforsvägen, 40
Bandhagen 12432, Sweden
+46 8647 7720
info@aps-sweden.com

Applied Scholastics Taiwan
8f 318
Fu-Hsing Road, Section 3
Taichumg, Taiwan
+886 2 276 99254
graemek2@yahoo.com

Applied Scholastics UK
59 Railway Approach
East Grinstead
West Sussex RH19 1BT
England
+44 1342 301 902
apsuk@AppliedScholastics.org

**Applied Scholastics
Western United States,**
P.O. Box 7424
Orange, CA 92867 USA
+1 714 538 3224
wuscontrep@AppliedScholastics.org

**Applied Scholastics
Zimbabwe**
PO Box 2156
Gweru, Midlands
Zimbabwe
+263 1174 9375
apsafrica@AppliedScholastics.org

---

www.AppliedScholastics.org
E-mail: education@AppliedScholastics.org